To: _____

From: _____

Published by The C. R. Gibson Company, Norwalk, CT 06856

ISBN 0-8378-5446-6
GB663

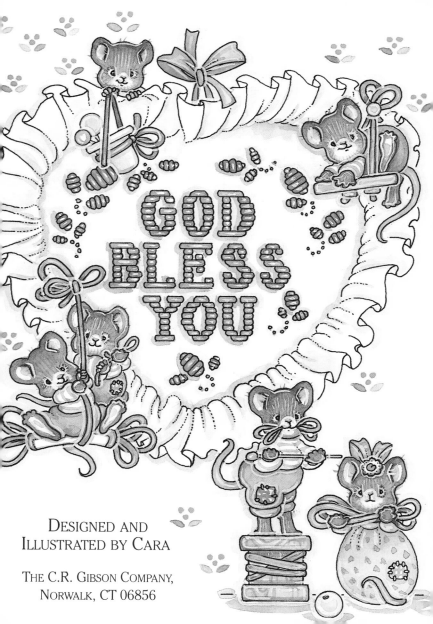

GOD BLESS YOU

DESIGNED AND
ILLUSTRATED BY CARA

THE C.R. GIBSON COMPANY,
NORWALK, CT 06856

# The Moon

I see the moon,
And the moon sees me;
God bless the moon,
And God bless me.

UNKNOWN

# The Lord's Prayer

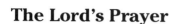

Our Father, who art in heaven,
Hallowed be Thy name.
Thy kingdom come;
Thy will be done
On earth as it is in heaven.
Give us this day our daily bread,
And forgive us our debts,
As we forgive our debtors.
And lead us not into temptation,
But deliver us from evil.
For Thine is the kingdom,
And the power, and the glory,
For ever.

New Testament

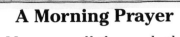

## A Morning Prayer

Father in Heaven, all through the night
I have been sleeping, safe in Thy sight.
Father, I thank Thee; bless me I pray,
Bless me and keep me all through the day.

AUTHOR UNKNOWN

## The Morning Bright

The morning bright,
With rosy light,
Has waked me from my sleep;
Father, I own,
    Thy love alone
      Thy little one doth keep.

THOMAS O. SUMMERS

## Lamb of God, I Look to Thee

Lamb of God, I look to Thee;
Thou shalt my example be;
Thou are gentle, meek, and mild,
Thou wast once a little child.

Loving Jesus, gentle Lamb,
In Thy gracious hands I am,
Make me, Savior, what Thou art,
Live Thyself within my heart.

CHARLES WESLEY

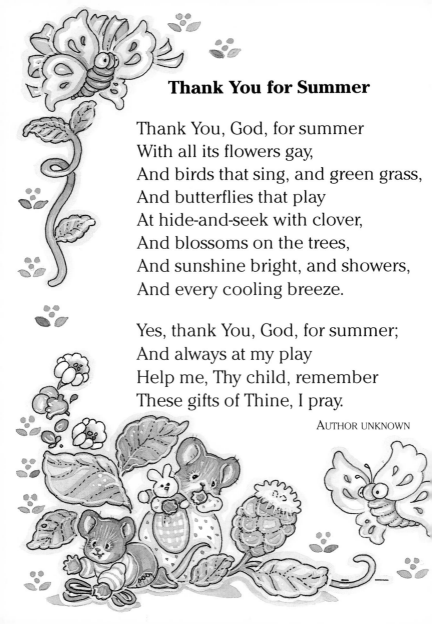

# Thank You for Summer

Thank You, God, for summer
With all its flowers gay,
And birds that sing, and green grass,
And butterflies that play
At hide-and-seek with clover,
And blossoms on the trees,
And sunshine bright, and showers,
And every cooling breeze.

Yes, thank You, God, for summer;
And always at my play
Help me, Thy child, remember
These gifts of Thine, I pray.

AUTHOR UNKNOWN

## God, We Thank You

God, we thank You for this food,
For rest and home and all things good;
For wind and rain and sun above,
But most of all for those we love.

MARYLEONA FROST

## Before I Run to Play

Now before I run to play,
Let me not forget to pray
To God who kept me through the night
And waked me with the morning light.

Help me, Lord, to love Thee more
Than I ever loved before,
In my work and in my play,
Be Thou with me through the day.

AUTHOR UNKNOWN

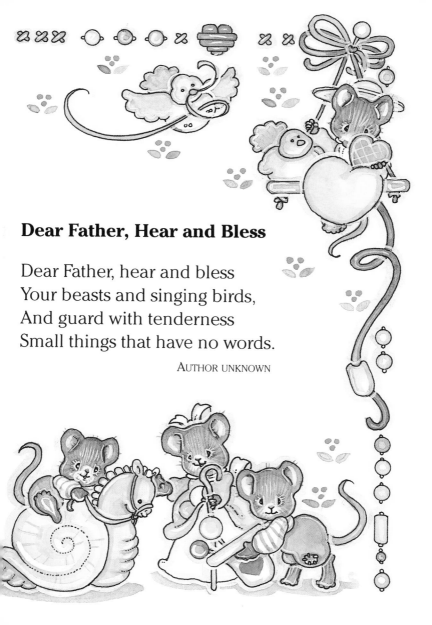

## Dear Father, Hear and Bless

Dear Father, hear and bless
Your beasts and singing birds,
And guard with tenderness
Small things that have no words.

AUTHOR UNKNOWN

Here a little child I stand
Heaving up my either hand.
Cold as toads though they be,
Here I lift them up to Thee,
For a blessing to fall
On our meat, and on us all.

ROBERT HERRICK

Thank you for the world so sweet,
Thank you for the food we eat.
Thank you for the birds that sing,
Thank you, God, for everything.

TRADITIONAL

# Praise God

Praise God, from whom all blessings flow;
Praise Him, all creatures here below;
Praise Him above, ye heavenly host:
Praise Father, Son, and Holy Ghost.

THOMAS KEN

Lord, make me an instrument of your peace
Where there is hatred, let me sow love;
Where there is injury, pardon;
Where there is doubt, faith;
Where there is despair, hope;
Where there is darkness, light;
Where there is sadness, joy.

ST. FRANCIS OF ASSISI

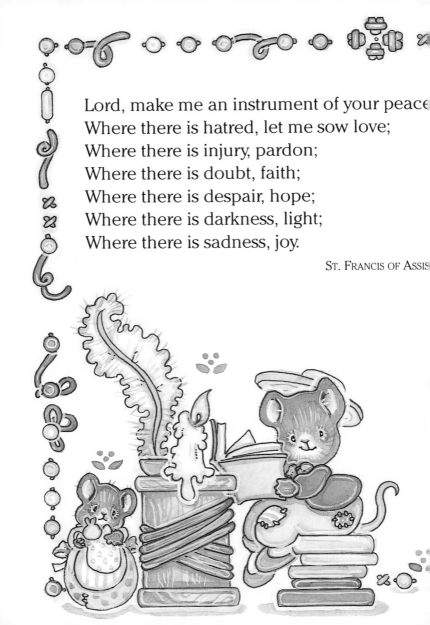

Lord of the loving heart,
May mine be loving too,
Lord of the gentle hands,
May mine be gentle too.
Lord of the willing feet,
May mine be willing too,
So may I grow more like thee
In all I say or do.

AUTHOR UNKNOWN

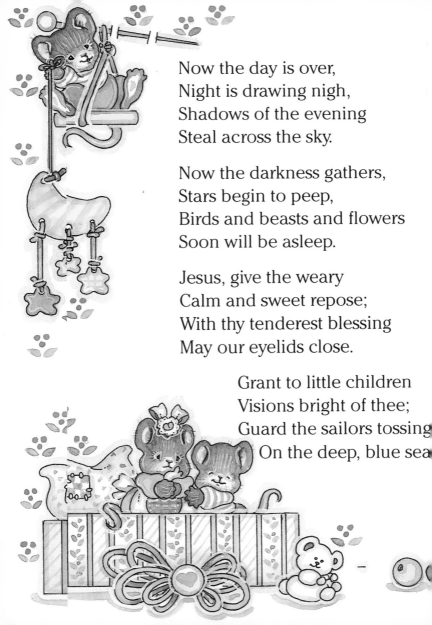

Now the day is over,
Night is drawing nigh,
Shadows of the evening
Steal across the sky.

Now the darkness gathers,
Stars begin to peep,
Birds and beasts and flowers
Soon will be asleep.

Jesus, give the weary
Calm and sweet repose;
With thy tenderest blessing
May our eyelids close.

Grant to little children
Visions bright of thee;
Guard the sailors tossing
On the deep, blue sea

When the morning wakens,
Then may I arise
Pure, and fresh, and sinless
In thy holy eyes.

S. BARING-GOULD

## Thou Art Great

Thou art great and Thou art good,
And we thank Thee for this food.
By Thy hand must all be fed,
And we thank Thee for this bread.

TRADITIONAL

# Now I Lay Me Down to Sleep

Now I lay me
   down to sleep,
I pray Thee, Lord,
   Thy child to keep;
Thy love go with me
   all the night,
And wake me with
   the morning light.

AUTHOR UNKNOWN

### Be Near Me, Lord Jesus

Be near me, Lord Jesus,
I ask Thee to stay,
Close by me forever,
and love me, I pray.
Bless all the dear children
in Thy tender care,
And take us to heaven,
to live with Thee there.

MARTIN LUTHER

He prayeth best,
Who loveth best
All things both
Great and small;
For the dear God
Who loveth us,
He made and loveth all.

SAMUEL TAYLOR COLERIDGE

## Dear God

Dear God,
Be good to me.
The sea is so wide
And my boat is so small.

PRAYER OF A FISHERMAN

# Good Night Prayer

Father, unto Thee I pray,
Thou hast guarded me all day;
Safe I am while in Thy sight,
Safely let me sleep tonight.

Bless my friends, the whole world bless;
Help me to learn helpfulness;
Keep me ever in Thy sight;
So to all I say good night.

HENRY JOHNSTONE

## Jesus, Tender Shepherd

Jesus, tender Shepherd, hear me;
Bless Thy little lamb tonight;
Through the darkness be Thou near me,
Keep me safe till morning light.

All this day Thy hand has led me,
And I thank thee for Thy care;
Thou has warmed me, clothed and fed me
Listen to my evening prayer.

Let my sins all be forgiven;
Bless the friends I love so well:
Take us all at last to heaven,
Happy there with Thee to dwell.

MARY DUNCAN

## Good Night

Good night! Good night!
Far flies the light;
But still God's love
Shall flame above,
Making all bright.
Good night! Good night!

VICTOR HUGO

# Father, We Thank Thee

For flowers that bloom about our feet,
Father, we thank Thee,
For tender grass so fresh and sweet,
Father, we thank Thee,
For the song of bird and hum of bee,
For all things fair we hear or see,
Father in heaven, we thank Thee.

For this new morning with its light,
Father, we thank Thee,
For rest and shelter of the night,
Father, we thank Thee,
For health and food, for love and friends,
For everything Thy goodness sends,
Father in heaven, we thank Thee.

RALPH WALDO EMERSON

God be in my head,
And in my understanding;

God be in my eyes,
And in my looking;

God be in my mouth,
And in my speaking;

God be in my heart,
And in my thinking;

God be at my end,
And at my departing.

SARUM MISSAL

Teach us, Lord;
To serve you as you deserve;
To give and not to count the cost;
To fight and not to heed the wounds;
To toil and not to seek for rest;
To labor and not to ask for any reward
Save that of knowing that we do your wil

ST. IGNATIUS LOYOL

## Cradle Song

Sweet dreams, form a shade
O'er my lovely infant's head;
Sweet dreams of pleasant streams
By happy, silent, moony beams.

WILLIAM BLAKE

Glory be to God for dappled things—
For skies of couple-colour
as a brinded cow;
For rose-moles all in stipple
upon trout that swim;
Fresh-firecoal chestnut-falls;
finches' wings;
Landscape plotted and
   pieced—fold, fallow, and plough;

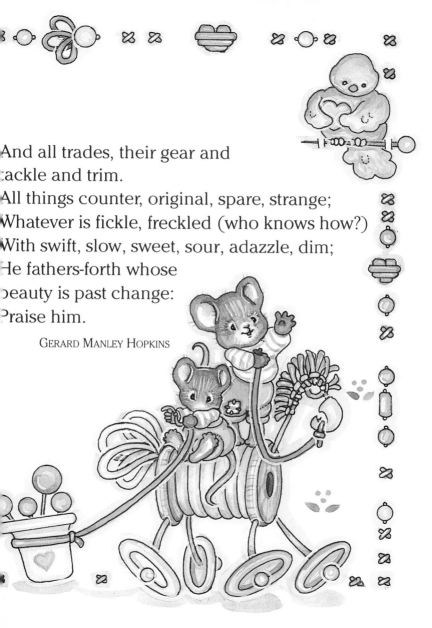

And all trades, their gear and
tackle and trim.
All things counter, original, spare, strange;
Whatever is fickle, freckled (who knows how?)
With swift, slow, sweet, sour, adazzle, dim;
He fathers-forth whose
beauty is past change:
Praise him.

GERARD MANLEY HOPKINS

## Grace Before Meals

Be present at our table, Lord;
Be here and everywhere adored.
Thy creatures bless, and grant that we
May feast in paradise with Thee.

JOHN WESLEY

## Bless Us, O Lord

Bless us, O Lord, for these Thy gifts
Which we are about to receive
From Thy bounty,
Through Christ our Lord.

TRADITIONAL

Matthew, Mark, Luke, and John,
Bless the bed that I lie on.
Before I lay me down to sleep
I give my soul to Christ to keep.
Four corners to my bed,
Four angels overspread:
One at the head, one at the feet,
And two to guard me while I sleep.
I go by sea, I go by land,
The Lord made me with His right hand,
If any danger come to me,
Sweet Jesus Christ, deliver me.
He is the branch and I'm the flower,
May God send me a happy hour.

TRADITIONAL

## Song

The year's at the spring
And day's at the morn;
Morning's at seven;
The hillside's dew-pearled;
The lark's on the wing;
The snail's on the thorn:
God's in His heaven—
All's right with the world!

ROBERT BROWNING

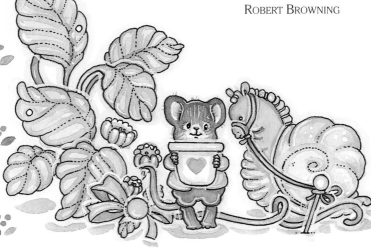

## North, South, East, and West

North, South, East, and West,
May Thy holy name be blessed;
Everywhere beneath the sun,
May Thy holy will be done.

WILLIAM CANTON

A little sparrow cannot fall
Unnoticed, Lord, by Thee;
And though I am so young and small
Thou dost take care of me.

JANE TAYLOR

I will lie down and sleep,
in peace. For you alone, Lord,
make me dwell in safety.

PSALMS 4:8